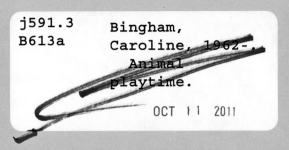

ANIMAL *playtime*

DK Publishing

LONDON, NEW YORK,
MELBOURNE, MUNICH, and DELHI

Written and edited by
Caroline Bingham and Fleur Star
Designed by Rachael Foster

US Editor Margaret Parrish
Production Editor Clare McLean
Production Controller Claire Pearson
Jacket Designer Gemma Fletcher
Art Director Martin Wilson
Publishing Manager Bridget Giles
Category Publisher Mary Ling

Consultant Kim Dennis-Bryan, PhD, FZS

First published in the United States in 2011 by
DK Publishing
375 Hudson Street, New York, New York 10014

11 12 13 14 15   10 9 8 7 6 5 4 3 2 1
001—181152—Jul/11

A catalog record for this book is available
from the Library of Congress.

ISBN: 978-0-7566-8226-2

Printed and bound in Singapore by
Star Standard Industries Pte. Ltd.

Discover more at
www.dk.com

Contents

Let's play!

What's your favorite time of day? Playtime! Animals like to play, too—but for them, it means more than just having fun. They learn all kinds of important skills through playing.

Getting a grip

For young monkeys, a forest is like a huge jungle gym. They learn to climb at a very young age. By the time they grow up, they can move through the trees with ease.

I didn't slip! I meant to hang by my tail, honest.

Running, jumping, climbing, pouncing,

Making friends

Lots of animals live in groups. The best way for them all to get along is to play together, just like you do with your friends.

You can't catch me

Many animals are hunted in the wild. Running for fun helps them to build up speed and practice dodges or other ways to keep from being caught.

Just for fun

When a dog chases a ball, it's using skills that wild dogs, such as foxes, need for hunting. Fox cubs learn to chase and pounce through play-fighting with other cubs.

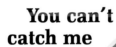

wrestling—how do you like to play?

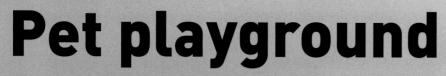

Pet playground

If you have a pet hamster, you'll know how much they love to play. They explore every corner of their burrow at night, always on the lookout for interesting snacks to pop into their cheeks.

I love to climb

Hamsters sleep all day and come out at night. They like a choice of objects to clamber over.

Yum, tasty!

Can you see me?

Keeping fit
A hamster wheel helps to keep
a hamster in shape, and it will
crawl through any tunnel it finds.

Crazy cats

Cats of all ages like to play and have lots of energy for running and chasing. Their play copies the way wild cats hunt for food.

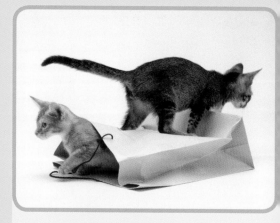

What's in here?
Cats are very curious and make a game of exploring boxes and bags. Sometimes a hidden cat will leap out at you from under a bedsheet!

Get ready... pounce!
When a cat spies something it wants to play with, it will crouch down to watch the toy. Then it will suddenly pounce to catch it.

Cats will play with all kinds of things.

I can catch that

Kittens and adult cats are like acrobats when chasing a toy. They can leap up high, stand up on their back legs, and roll on their backs.

Mom, wake up! I want to play.

I want to play

Kittens tend to play more often than adult cats, just the same as children play more than their parents.

I found it!

Play is an important part of a dog's day. Pet dogs enjoy chasing toys to bring them back.

Ball games
Puppies and adult dogs all like to play, usually with other dogs or people. Their games include chasing and play-fights.

When a dog wags its tail, it is

Please play with me

Dogs can't use words, but they can let you know when they want to play. They go down on their front legs and wag their tails.

It's mine!

Disc competitions for dogs are very popular in some parts of the world. These dogs both want to be the first to bring the disc back.

showing you it is happy.

Leaping lambs

Young lambs are very playful. They have lots of energy to run and jump. They like to explore and even climb on top of each other to see what's going on.

Stop bouncing around. It's time for dinner.

Lambs like to jump and play, but

Play nicely

Like you, lambs can get excited when they play with their friends. Sometimes they end up headbutting each other!

Flock together

Sheep prefer to spend time in groups, which are called flocks. Lambs often follow a leader, and they get upset if they're left on their own.

Thanks for the piggyback ride, Mom!

adult sheep prefer to eat or nap.

Just horsing around

Baby horses, called foals, love to play when they are not eating or sleeping (and they sleep a lot!). Playing is how foals learn about their world.

Horses enjoy rolling on the ground—it's the best way for them to scratch their backs and stretch out. This foal thinks its mom is ready to play and wants to join in.

I'm going for a run
A foal will play with its mom and with other foals, but will also race around on its own, stretching its legs and running just for the fun of it.

When it's not playing, a newborn foal

Let's let Mom eat!

Foals from different moms will happily play with each other if they are brought up together. This leaves their mothers free to graze.

Horses hate to be alone and form friendships that can last a lifetime. They groom each other as an important part of this friendship.

spends about half its day sleeping.

Duck rides

Ducklings can swim within a few hours of being born. But just like a small child learning to walk, they can get too tired to move.

Scoot up! You've got more room in front and I'm falling off the back.

Mom to the rescue

These Merganser ducklings are worn out from swimming all day. The journey to shore is just too far, so they get a lift home from Mom.

Merganser ducklings dive for their own

All aboard!

Young swans, called cygnets, take to the water when they are a day old. At the first sign of danger, they hop onto Mom's back and hide safely under her wings.

food when they're just one day old.

Fox cub fun

Arctic foxes have large litters. With seven or more brothers and sisters, a young fox has a lot of playmates.

Fox cubs spend a lot of time rolling and tumbling. After a hard day's play, they all curl up together to sleep.

Let's settle down for a quick nap and then we can play some more.

Arctic foxes have a brown summer

I've got you!

Through play-fighting, fox cubs pick up skills they will use when hunting. They also learn how to defend themselves.

This is a good game... and I can jump higher than you!

Ready, aim, pounce!

In the depths of winter, an Arctic fox hunts by listening for animals under the snow and pouncing. Cubs copy the pouncing when they play.

coat and a white winter coat.

Polar playground

In the frozen Arctic, polar bears have to make their own fun. Young cubs are very curious and like to explore. Even adults enjoy rolling around on the ice.

Cub battles
Male polar bears have play-fights to show who's boss. When young cubs wrestle, they are copying the older bears.

Young cubs have lots of energy to keep

Don't wake Mom!
A cub usually has one or two brothers and sisters. They are perfect playmates for rough and tumble games—such as using Mom as a jungle gym!

Why should cubs have all the fun?

up with Mom as she looks for food.

Riding the waves

With long, sleek bodies and powerful tails, dolphins are born to swim! They speed through the water in groups, and have lots of fun as they go.

Surf's up!

It's not just people who like surfing! Dolphins enjoy leaping out of the water to ride on a wave. They also swim alongside boats so they can jump through the waves the boats churn up.

Whee! We don't need surfboards to ride the waves.

Roll over

Even though they are large animals, dolphins can turn a whole somersault. They push themselves out of the water with their tails and twist around in the air.

Water toys

Dolphins are smart. Just like you, they enjoy doing different things so they don't get bored. They play with seaweed, chase turtles, and play-fight with other dolphins.

Fun in the forest

Young raccoons are as playful as kittens. They like to roll around and play-fight with their brothers and sisters in their forest home.

Oops-a-daisy!
Raccoons are expert climbers. Kits develop their balance by exploring in trees—but it doesn't always go well! Kits can slip as they try to pass each other on the same branch.

Young raccoons are called kits.

Raccoon moms usually have between three and seven kits.

Is someone coming? Quick, let's hide!

Room for all

A lot of raccoons must fit inside one den. They shelter inside hollow trees and in underground burrows, and even come inside people's sheds.

King of the castle

Mountain goats are happiest on rocky slopes. Baby goats, called kids, quickly learn to jump and leap and climb through playing.

Take that!
Young goats like to practice headbutting. Some like it more than others!

Mountain goats are closely

I can fly!
Goats have no fear of heights and will jump across large gaps in the rocks with ease. Their hooves have special flexible pads that help them to grip.

Can I make it?
A young goat is able to make big leaps, but will always investigate first. This goat is looking for a way to climb a boulder larger than he is.

related to antelope.

I've got you!

Otters are incredibly playful. They like to play chase with other otters—when they're not busy sliding down muddy banks or snowy slopes.

Caught you! Now it's your turn. Try to catch me!

Otters are very curious and like

Speeding along

Otters enjoy running, but tobogganing is even more fun. They slide along on their stomachs before diving into the water with a splash.

Let's see who can dive the deepest.

Playing together

Most otters live in familes, and they form close bonds. Otters like jumping on their brothers and sisters and rolling over in pretend fights.

In the water

Otters spend a lot of time in rivers and lakes hunting for fish, crabs, and crayfish. They also like to duck and dive with each other just for fun.

to explore their riverbank homes.

Time for a rest

Capybaras spend most of their time relaxing with their big family group. To talk to each other, they bark, grunt, whistle, and purr.

That was a nice nap. Now it's hot, so I'm ready to go swimming.

Capybaras can swim just a few

Splashing around

Capybaras spend lots of their time diving and swimming. Their eyes, ears, and noses are high up on their heads. This means they can see, hear, and smell while they are swimming.

Ok, let's go. We can eat some grass later.

Chilling out

On a hot afternoon, capybaras cool off in rivers and lakes. They laze around in the water for hours with their parents, brothers, and sisters. In the evening, they go to find food.

hours after they are born.

It's a bear's life

A mother bear usually has between one and four cubs. Cubs play with Mom as much as they can, but brothers and sisters will spend hours playing together.

Water fights
While these cubs enjoy splashing each other, they are also learning adult behavior. Adults will protect their catch of fish if another bear gets too close.

In addition to climbing trees, bears

It's mine!

A bear has powerful jaws. If two cubs want to play with the same stick, they'll both try their hardest to keep it.

Oh no, I've climbed so high I don't know how to get back down!

Up we go

Bears are excellent climbers, but sometimes the cubs will get a bit stuck. Going up is easy. Climbing back down is a little bit harder.

also like to play in rivers and lakes.

Look behind you!

Meerkats live in gangs of up to 30 adults and pups. Adults take turns looking after the young pups, who are always busy playing.

What's that over there?

I'm gonna get you while the babysitter's not looking!

Building bonds

When living in a big group, it's important for everyone to get along. Playing helps pups to make friends and build trust.

On guard

Meerkats are always alert for danger, even while they sunbathe to get warm. Full of energy, pups prefer to look for insects instead.

Meerkats live in deserts in Africa.

Spot the cheetah

Cheetahs hunt over large areas of grassland. Cubs need to learn to spot, chase, and attack prey, and practice on each other.

Fighting tooth and claw
Cheetahs trip up their prey with their claws and then attack it with their teeth. Wrestling cubs copy these moves—but more gently!

Like many animals, cubs learn

Cheetahs are the fastest mammals on land. When they chase prey, they can run as fast as cars on a highway, but only for up to 20 seconds. Prey may escape if it can keep running for longer.

Family ties

Cheetah moms can have three or four cubs. Young cheetahs leave their mother before they are 20 months old, but brothers can stay together for their whole lives.

Can you see any prey from up there? I want to look!

by copying their parents.

A day of play

Young chimpanzees are just like children. They can spend a whole day playing games with their friends. Adults like to play, too, because it helps them make friends within their group.

Time out
Favorite chimp games include swinging on branches, chasing, and wrestling. After a hard day's play, chimps head to the trees and make a nest of leaves to rest in.

Chimps enjoy being tickled and can

Let's go faster!

Most chimps have one baby, but some have twins. Young chimps ride around on Mom's back until they are five years old. Then Mom will have a new baby to carry around.

Chimpanzees are primates (a kind of mammal). All monkeys and apes are primates—and so are people. In fact, chimps are our nearest animal relatives. This is why they sometimes act just like us.

Can you see food?

These young chimps peer inside a termite mound to find some tasty termites to eat. They learn this and many other actions by copying adults and turning it into a game.

even laugh. It sounds like panting.

I love throwing water and mud around with my trunk. Did I splash you?

Elephants live in hot places, such as India and Africa. They love mud pools. Mud acts as nature's sunscreen. It adds a protective layer to their skin, helping to stop sunburn and prevent insect bites.

Playing in the mud

Elephants like to spend time together, and moms and babies share messy mud baths. It's lots of fun and keeps them healthy.

Elephants live in groups called herds. They all help each other. If a baby elephant gets stuck in mud, it's not long before an adult or two will help it out.

I'm going to win this trunk—wrestling game!

Mud, glorious mud
Does your mom get mad when you get muddy? Elephant moms don't! They teach their babies to roll in the mud as a way to keep cool in the hot sun.

Elephants use their long trunks to smell and to introduce themselves. They also use them to play games of trunk wrestling or tug-of-war.

Caught you!

Lion cubs need to learn to hunt. This is how they will catch their food when they grow up. They gain hunting skills through wrestling and chasing other cubs—but they don't really hurt each other.

Finding their role

Female adult lions hunt in a team. Some lionesses chase the prey, and others kill it. When cubs wrestle each other, it helps them find out which job they would do best.

Come here!

Just like small cats, lion cubs love to chase anything that moves. This is good practice for finding and chasing prey in the wide, open grasslands where they live.

There's always someone for

Lions are the only big cats that live in groups, called prides. There are usually between four and six female lions in a pride. Each mom can have up to six cubs, so there are lots of cubs to play with.

You can try to hold me back Dad, but I'll bite!

a cub to play with in a pride.

Monkey business

There can be up to 60 baboons of all ages in a troop. The young members spend a lot of their time playing.

Time to groom
Baboons, like all monkeys, spend time grooming each other. It's a way to show friendship.

Whee! I like playing leapfrog!

Baboons talk to each other using

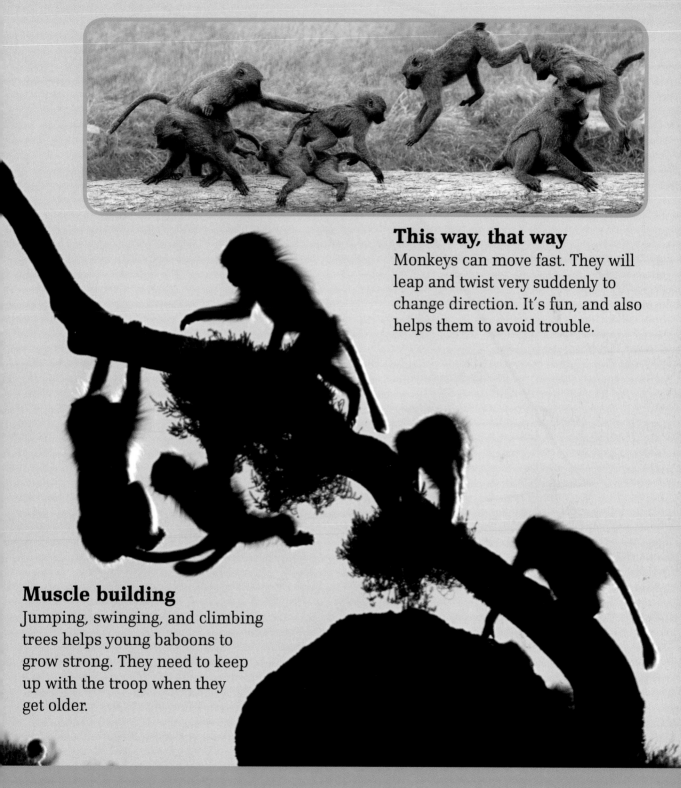

This way, that way

Monkeys can move fast. They will leap and twist very suddenly to change direction. It's fun, and also helps them to avoid trouble.

Muscle building

Jumping, swinging, and climbing trees helps young baboons to grow strong. They need to keep up with the troop when they get older.

barks, grunts, clicks, and calls.

Pandas at play

Giant pandas eat mostly bamboo. This doesn't give them much energy, but they still love to play!

Mom, I think you're having even more fun than I am!

Panda moms have been known

What shall we play?

Giant pandas live alone in the wild, but in panda centers cubs might live together. They like wrestling and tumbling with each other and even share toys.

It's a long way down. I'm glad I have sharp claws to hang on!

Climbing trees

Much of the time, pandas like to sleep. They shelter in trees, so cubs quickly learn how to climb. They can scramble up a tree when they are just six months old.

These black and white bears live in mountain forests in China. They are very rare and need protecting. There are more pandas being looked after in conservation centers than there are in the wild.

to wake up their cubs to play.

Hanging around

Orangutans usually live alone, but when youngsters are brought together in refuges, they love to play. They tickle and chase each other, have play-fights, and roll around for hours at a time.

Is this a good umbrella?
Some animals use tools. Orangutans have found that large leaves make useful umbrellas to keep them dry when it rains. They hate to get wet!

At night, orangutans make

A tight grip

Orangutan babies stay with Mom until they are about eight years old. They are happy in their treetop homes from a young age, thanks to strong arms and feet that can grasp.

sleeping nests from branches.

Hop, skip, and jump

When it's time for a group of sifakas to move, they all travel together through the forests of Madagascar. It's a bouncy ride for a baby clinging to its mother's back!

 Sifakas spend most of their time in the

Getting to know you

When two sifakas meet, they may attack each other. This is less likely if they get to know each other. The best way to do this is through a game of wrestling or a massage.

My long legs, arms, and tail help me keep my balance.

Do the locomotion

Sifakas are expert at climbing trees, but aren't so good at walking. Instead they bound along the ground. Huge strides help them cover enormous distances very quickly.

treetops, leaping from trunk to trunk.

Let's make snowballs

Japanese macaques live high up in the snow-covered mountains and forests of Japan. They really know how to have fun in the winter!

Having a ball
Young macaques enjoy rolling snow into balls. They carry the snowballs around and stand on them, but don't throw them.

Japanese macaques are also

This is MY snowball. No one will take it away from me!

Play nicely

Up to 100 macaques live in a troop, so there are always lots of friends to play with. Moms and dads share in looking after all the youngsters.

It's cold out here!

It gets very cold in the mountains in winter. To warm up, macaques sit in the water or steam from hot springs. It's like having a hot bath on a cold day.

called snow monkeys.

These two sea lions are playing chase.

Sea lions use their strong front flippers to move their bodies through the water.

Surfing sea lions

Sea lions live in large groups and spend quite a lot of time playing in the water. They are known for being smart and have good memories.

You won't catch me—I can dodge out of your way!

Sea lions close their ears

Surfing the waves

Sea lions seem to enjoy surfing in breaking waves, just like people enjoy body surfing. Groups will gather to play together.

I'm an acrobat

On land, sea lions are a little bit clumsy, but in the sea their bodies are the perfect shape to cut through the water with ease.

and nostrils when they dive.

Easy does it

Koalas don't have much energy or time for playing—they spend 18 hours asleep every day! The rest of the time, they eat.

I wish I could escape to my own tree and have some peace and quiet.

Group hug

Wild koalas live alone, but only where there are other koalas. But koalas in refuges seem to like spending lots of time with others.

56

Koalas live in eucalyptus forests in

In the trees

Koalas spend most of their time in trees. They climb slowly through treetops to find leaves to eat and can jump from trunk to trunk.

Time to move

A baby koala is called a joey. It spends its first six months inside its mother's pouch. Then it clings to her back for the next six months as she moves around the trees.

Australia.

Ready, set, go!

Penguins, such as these Adélies, live in large colonies.
They can often be spotted playing follow the leader.
Where one goes, the rest will follow.

Wait for me!

Here we go.
Flippers back,
head down...

Ready to leap

Penguins rest on ice, but have to enter
the water to find food. They often make
a leap and dive in, which looks like fun.

Adélies leap over the waves,

Tobogganing

Penguins walk slowly, but sliding along on their bellies is much faster. They also seem to enjoy it.

Keep up! Lie on your stomach and push with your feet.

This is fun! Now let's find some fish.

just like dolphins.

Making friends

Wild animals usually play with others in their own group—it's safest that way. But pets often meet different animals, and some become fast friends.

Will you be my friend?

Horses are "herd animals"—in the wild, they live in groups. If a horse has no other horses around, it will find another animal to bond with. Dogs do this, too.

Animals need to trust each

Come on, Tortoise. I want to go faster!

Young kittens like to explore. This one has never met a tortoise before and has climbed on top to check it out. If the kitten felt the tortoise were a threat, it would run away.

I'm going as fast as I can!

other to play together.

Glossary

When you're learning about animals, it helps to know the meanings of some special words you'll find in this book.

colony a large group of animals (such as penguins) that lives closely together.

conservation the protection of a particular area and the living things it contains.

cygnet a young swan. Cygnets have gray feathers. Adult swans have white feathers.

flipper a flattened limb. Sea lions have flippers, as do dolphins.

flock a group of sheep or birds that lives together.

foal a horse that is less than one year old.

grooming when an animal cleans its fur or another animal's fur.

herd a large group of hoofed animals that lives or travels together.

hunt the way in which an animal follows its prey.

kit a baby racoon.

litter the name given to a group of newborn animals, such as kittens, that are born to the same mother.

prey an animal that is hunted for food.

pride a group of lions that lives and hunts together.

refuge an animal refuge is a place of safety, where injured animals are cared for and rare animals are protected.

troop a group of monkeys.

Playing is one of the best ways

Bye, bye! I hope you've learned a lot about the different ways we like to play.

Picture credits

The publisher would like to thank the following for their kind permission to reproduce their photographs: (Key: a-above; b-below/bottom; c-center; f-far; l-left; r-right; t-top)

Alamy Images: AfriPics.com 35; Arco Images GmbH/C. Huetter 5t, 36-37; blickwinkel/Schmidbauer 22-23; Penny Boyd 45t; Mike Cooper 29cr; Holger Ehlers 31br; Patrick J. Endres 58-59; Don Grall/Danita Delimont 59br; Ellen Isaacs 11br; Ernie Janes 13b; Gavriel Jecan/ Danita Delimont 31t; Juniors Bildarchiv/F314 6-7, 7br; Juniors Bildarchiv/F248 28-29; Juniors Bildarchiv/ F259 6cl; Juniors Bildarchiv/F315 60cla; Juniors Bildarchiv/F393 11tr; Juniors Bildarchiv/R304 14cl; Peter Lewis 13tr; Wayne Lynch/All Canada Photos 19b; Barrie Neil 34; Photoshot Holdings Ltd 44b; David & Micha Sheldon/F1online digitale Bildagentur GmbH 16-17; Darron R. Silva/Aurora Photos 57cl; Peter Steiner 25; Top-Pics TBK 14-15; T. Ulrich/ClassicStock 24l; Maximilian Weinzierl 7tr; WILDLIFE GmbH 15tr, 57tl; Konrad Wothe/Imagebroker 8b. **Corbis**: AlaskaStock 21b; Theo Allofs 55t; DLILLC 29tl; W. Wayne Lockwood, M.D. 27tr; Roberta Olenick/All Canada Photos 26cl, 26-27; John Pitcher/Design Pics 24cr; Paul A. Souders 35tl. **FLPA**: Ingo Arndt/Minden Pictures 4, 42cr; Stephen Belcher/Minden Pictures 53cr; Gerry Ellis/Minden Pictures 1, 40, 41tr, 41cl, 41crb; Suzi Eszterhas/Minden Pictures 49l, 49r; John Eveson 12-13; Katherine Feng/Minden Pictures 47tl; Sumio Harada/Minden Pictures 27cr; Michio Hoshino/ Minden Pictures 19t; ImageBroker 60bl, 60-61; Mitsuaki Iwago/Minden Pictures 5c, 53l, 56; Thomas Marent/Minden Pictures 62, 63; Yva Momatiuk & John Eastcott/Minden Pictures 32; Elliot Neep 3; Cyril Ruoso/Minden Pictures 50; Jurgen & Christine Sohns 25tr; Terry Whittaker 23tr; Konrad Wothe/Minden Pictures 9r, 52cr, 53tr; ZSSD/ Minden Pictures 42clb, 46. **Getty Images**: China Span/ Keren Su 47r; Digital Vision/Karl Ammann 39b; Flickr/ Photo by PJ Taylor 10-11; Fuse 54-55, 59t; The Image Bank/Daniel J. Cox 2; National Geographic/Michael Nichols 38, 44-45; National Geographic/Norbert Rosing 18, 33tl; Panoramic Images 37br; Riser/Keren Su 52l; Riser/Kevin Schafer 37tr; Riser/Paul Souders 32cr; Robert Harding World Imagery/Thorsten Milse 21tl; Workbook Stock/Jami Tarris 44cra. **National Geographic Stock**: Suzi Eszterhas/Minden Pictures 42-43. **naturepl.com**: Jane Burton 9cl; Chris Gomersall 33r; Steven Kazlowski 20; Inaki Relanzon 50c, 51cl, 51c, 51cr; Anup Shah 39tr, 48; Dave Watts 57r. **Photolibrary**: Juniors Bildarchiv 14bl; Morales Morales 30-31; OSF/Mary Plage 55b; OSF/Owen Newman 18tr; Ronald Wittek 17t. **SeaPics.com**: George Jiri Karbus 23crb. **Specialist Stock/Still Pictures**: Biosphoto/Cyril Ruoso 51tr. **Warren Photographic**: 5b.

Jacket images: *Front*: **Alamy Images**: Mark Newman/Alaska Stock LLC. *Back*: **FLPA**: Gerry Ellis/ Minden Pictures tl. **Getty Images**: The Image Bank/ Eastcott Momatiuk.

All other images © Dorling Kindersley
For further information see: www.dkimages.com

to learn new things!

Index

DK Publishing would like to thank Jemma Westing and Rob Nunn.